Mexican Word of the Day

Edited by: Rafael Marquez

ISBN: 978-1-257-79712-7
©2008, 2011 Marquez Publishing
All Rights Reserved

Hi,

These are jokes folks, so no need to get all offended by it.

To really get the full effect, it may help if you know a few words of Spanish, or if you live somewhere where they speak Spanish, but regardless, I think these are quite hilarious.

Let me give you a little bit of background on how I got to this point.

Basically, middle of the year 2008, I posted an article with some of these words on my blog. The response to that post was overwhelming. I've had a consistent 200-300 visitors a day to this one article.

Many of the visitors read the words of the day and also left their own words of the day in the comments. I had to clean some of the words up since they were a bit off color, but maybe in a future revision I'll include the uncensored versions.

I had the idea to put together a compilation of the words into a printed book for about 18 months now, but never quite found the motivation to see it through. I don't know who originally came up with the concept of "The Mexican Word of the Day," I just feel in love with the concept of it. For the record, I'm Venezuelan and my girlfriend is Mexican.

Enjoy!

Rafael Marquez - Editor

MEXICAN WORD OF THE DAY: WAFER

I wanted to go to the movies with my friends; pero the mensos didn't wafer me.

Rafael Marquez – Editor

MEXICAN WORD OF THE DAY: JULY
Ju told me ju were going to tha store and JULY to me! JULYER

MEXICAN WORD OF THE DAY: Mushroom

Orale vato, when all my family gets in the car there's not MUSHROOM!

pero - however

MEXICAN WORD OF THE DAY: C HICKEN
My wife wanted me to go to the store, pero CHICKEN go by herself.

MEXICAN WORD OF THE DAY: RECTUM

I had 2 cars but not anymore because my wife RECTUM both.

Rafael Marquez – Editor

MEXICAN WORD OF THE DAY: Texas

My ruca always TEXAS me when I leave the casa, wondering where I'm at.

MEXICAN WORD OF THE DAY: DEFENDER

Last week my ruca wrecked my car. Pero gracias a dios nothing happen 2 tha grill just DEFENDER.

Rafael Marquez – Editor

MEXICAN WORD OF THE DAY: JUAREZ

My vieja slapped me because she caught me looking at a chic walking by and I said, JUAREZ your freaking problem?

MEXICAN WORD OF THE DAY: CHEESE

My girlfriend wants me to get her pregnant pero CHEESE crazy!

Rafael Marquez – Editor

MEXICAN WORD OF THE DAY: BRIEF

My homie farted so bad that I couldn't BRIEF.

MEXICAN WORD OF THE DAY: CASHEW

I tried running after you but I couldn't CASHEW!

Rafael Marquez – Editor

MEXICAN WORD OF THE DAY: WATER

My vieja gets mad and I don't even know WATER problem is.

MEXICAN WORD OF THE DAY: THIRSTY

We still on for THIRSTY?

Rafael Marquez – Editor

MEXICAN WORD OF THE DAY: URINE

I was waiting in line at the grocery store, when my ruca yelled out, "URINE the wrong line pendejo!"

Alternate usage: Muevete a la chingada, URINE my way.

MEXICAN WORD OF THE DAY: PASTURIZE

Yo vato, that bullet almost hit you. It went right PASTURIZE.

Rafael Marquez – Editor

MEXICAN WORD OF THE DAY: RACIST

My homie and I were late getting to the race track. My homes got pissed and said: "I told you we shoulda left earlier cabron, the RACIST started!"

MEXICAN WORD OF THE DAY: Extinct

Whenever my ruca and I finish doing it, EXTINCTS like foot and ass.

Alternate usage: Change your chones, EXTINCT like pacuso (pata, culo y sudor).

MEXICAN WORD OF THE DAY: STUNNA

My ruca came in to get the kids, she asked: "Where are they?" I said "STUNNA."

MEXICAN WORD OF THE DAY: DISNEY

I went to the doctor's today. He asked "where does it hurt?" I said "DISNEY."

Rafael Marquez – Editor

MEXICAN WORD OF THE DAY: DEODORANT

I ate too many frijoles so I opened the window, but DEODORANT gone yet.

MEXICAN WORD OF THE DAY: BISHOP

The other day my ruca fell down the stairs and I had to pick the BISHOP.

MEXICAN WORD OF THE DAY: W<small>HEELCHAIR</small>

My homie was drinkin a beer so I asked him "hey vato where's mine?" He told me "this is the last one, but don't worry WHEELCHAIR"

MEXICAN WORD OF THE DAY: BODYWASH

I can't go out with the girls tonight because no BODYWASH my kids!

Rafael Marquez – Editor

MEXICAN WORD OF THE DAY: SHOULDER

My tia wanted to become a US citizen, but she didn't know how to read, so I SHOULDER.

MEXICAN WORD OF THE DAY: C HINO

I farted in bed the other night, but my girlfriend, CHINO like it.

MEXICAN WORD OF THE DAY: SODAS

My vieja likes to go on rollercoasters and SODAS her sister.

MEXICAN WORD OF THE DAY: PIKACHU

I took my kids to payless shoes and after walking around for an hour I said PIKACHU already!

Alternate usage: I was looking at my neighbor's vieja changing when she turn around and saw me. I say, "HEY I SWEAR I DIDN'T SEE NOTHING. I DIDN'T PIKACHU!"

Rafael Marquez – Editor

MEXICAN WORD OF THE DAY: HERPES

Me and my old lady went out to eat pizza. I got my piece and she got HERPES!

MEXICAN WORD OF THE DAY: FECES

I've been standing all day, and my FECES hurt.

Rafael Marquez – Editor

MEXICAN WORD OF THE DAY: DEFENSE
My neighbor's pet bull got loose so I had to jump DEFENSE.

MEXICAN WORD OF THE DAY: H̲ARASSMENT

Mi esposa caught me with another woman. I had to tell her that HARASSMENT nothing to me.

Rafael Marquez – Editor

MEXICAN WORD OF THE DAY: BUTTER and LETTUCE

My girl and I wanna get married BUTTER parents won't LETTUCE.

MEXICAN WORD OF THE DAY: Horchata
You can doo eet my way, HORCHATA hell up!

Rafael Marquez – Editor

MEXICAN WORD OF THE DAY: JUDO

A Homie gets in a fight for his life. He backs away from his opponent, takes a Martial Arts stance and says: "Watch out Ese, I know Mexican JUDO!"

Opponent laughingly replies: "What do you mean, Mexican JUDO?"

Homie's responds: "Pendejo, JUDO know if I gotta knife or if I gotta a gun!"

MEXICAN WORD OF THE DAY: DISPERSE

DISPERSE are going to beat the Lakers LOL! (a Texas special!)

Rafael Marquez – Editor

MEXICAN WORD OF THE DAY: M‍ARIJUANA
MARIJUANA go to the store ese?

MEXICAN WORD OF THE DAY: Highway

I turned over in bed last night and saw my wife with no makeup on... I said HIGHWAY you scared me!

Rafael Marquez – Editor

MEXICAN WORD OF THE DAY: HOOCHIE

My ruca found some other girls phone number in my pocket and said "you tell me HOOCHIE is cabron!"

MEXICAN WORD OF THE DAY: LEMONADE

Chale bato de espurs got LEMONADED by the Lakers

MEXICAN WORD OF THE DAY: PUTA

PUTA phone down and get back to work!

MEXICAN WORD OF THE DAY: CHICKENBONE

My girl was on her period for like a week, but not anymore.
CHICKENBONE now.

Rafael Marquez – Editor

MEXICAN WORD OF THE DAY: HEATER

When my leetle sister started to shoke, my mom told me to HEATER on the back.

MEXICAN WORD OF THE DAY: JUICY

Oye, I'll drive, pero I don't have inchurance...so tell me if JUICY the cops.

Rafael Marquez – Editor

MEXICAN WORD OF THE DAY: CHINOS

My ruca thinks CHINOS everything. But CHINOS nothing.

MEXICAN WORD OF THE DAY: DELL

You DELL him. No you DELL him. Chingao, someone's gotta DELL him.

MEXICAN WORD OF THE DAY: TOTEM

My wife and kids saw me with the anutter vieja, pero I just TOTEM "it wasn't me!"

MEXICAN WORD OF THE DAY: CHIEF

Chingao, I really hate driving that taco truck. Jew can never CHIEF it out of first gear.

Rafael Marquez – Editor

MEXICAN WORD OF THE DAY: HEAD LICE

"The cops pulled over my homeboy cuz one of his HEAD LICE were broken"

MEXICAN WORD OF THE DAY: BICHON FRISE

"My girlfriend didn't pay the heating bill. For all I care that BICHON FRISE"

MEXICAN WORD OF THE DAY: PICTURE

"I caught my old man with another woman! I told him to pick me or PICTURE!"

MEXICAN WORD OF THE DAY: HOUSE SHOE

"I saw that girl doing a backflip, and i asked her HOUSE SHOE do that?"

MEXICAN WORD OF THE DAY: ANDRES

Aye mamita, take off your clothes and ANDRES yourself for me.

MEXICAN WORD OF THE DAY: JESUS

My homie got all bent out of shape when my girl was making fun of em. I had to tell em JESUS playing with you homes.

Rafael Marquez – Editor

MEXICAN WORD OF THE DAY: SUBWAY

I saw my homie at the mall the other day. He said orale way! I told him SUBWAY!

MEXICAN WORD OF THE DAY: BEACH and SOCCER
If that BEACH doesn't stop talking shit, I'm gonna SOCCER!

MEXICAN WORD OF THE DAY: DIME

I don't know what DIME it is.

MEXICAN WORD OF THE DAY: CHILE

I asked my mom if I would go to the movies and CHILE me go.

Rafael Marquez – Editor

MEXICAN WORD OF THE DAY: HOTELS

Me and me amigo were on a secret mission but me amigo saw a girl that wanted to help and I said "no that HOTELS everyone everything!"

MEXICAN WORD OF THE DAY: LIVER and CHEESE
Me and my ruca were walking down the street one day and a vato whistled at her. I said liver alone cheese mine.

MEXICAN WORD OF THE DAY: PAKISTAN

One day, my padresito asked me: "Mijo, donde estan las llaves?" I said "PAKISTAN."

MEXICAN WORD OF THE DAY: T̲issue

Hey pendejo! If you dunno how to do that, lemme TISSUE!

Rafael Marquez – Editor

MEXICAN WORD OF THE DAY: Bicho & Damas

My borracho uncle was talking shit to me and I told him to chill cabron before I BICHO DAMAS UP!

MEXICAN WORD OF THE DAY: PORNO

My leetle bro bought a taco but he wouldn't chair with me. Then he started to shoke, n I told him ya ves pendejo PORNO darme!

MEXICAN WORD OF THE DAY: SHIPS

I went to the store to pick up some SHIPS and dip for the Super bowl party.

MEXICAN WORD OF THE DAY: TOPIC

My moms was trying on a bunch of dresses and I toll her TOPIC one and go - y ya!

MEXICAN WORD OF THE DAY: HERSHEYS

One of my employees is always coming in late, so I told her that she better straighten up HERSHEYS gone!

MEXICAN WORD OF THE DAY: CASINO

Mi primo left his novia CASINO like that lying perra.

MEXICAN WORD OF THE DAY: L̃iquor & Poker

I asked my carnal for some sex tips. He said, "LIQOUR in the front, POKER in the rear."

MEXICAN WORD OF THE DAY: WASHING

Yesterday at work, every time I looked up the stupidvisor was WASHING me.

MEXICAN WORD OF THE DAY: BIDET

I wanted to take my ruca on a trip to the beautiful city of Boston, BIDET all a bunch of whiney complainers coz dare quarterback got hurt!

MEXICAN WORD OF THE DAY: ANALYZE

Ana told everyone that I farted real stinky, pero don't believe her por que ANALYZE!!

MEXICAN WORD OF THE DAY: WATER

"hey vato WATER you doing"

MEXICAN WORD OF THE DAY: OBAMA

Last night my wife got mad at me cuz i drank her last case of beer OBAMA self!

Rafael Marquez – Editor

MEXICAN WORD OF THE DAY: JUPITER

My kids were acting bad at the store so I had to tell them JUPITER behave dammit or I'm gonna kick your ass when we get home!

MEXICAN WORD OF THE DAY: CHEATING

"Orale Vato, I think dos enchiladas were bad yesterday, ever since I ate dem I been CHEATING my brains out!

Rafael Marquez – Editor

MEXICAN WORD OF THE DAY: ACOUSTIC

Pedro started a fight in the bar last night, and I had to hit this guy with ACOUSTIC.

MEXICAN WORD OF THE DAY: SHERIFF

Excuse me Osifer!! I'm not gonna give you some of my cerveza BITCH!!! I don't have to SHERIFF I don't want to.

Rafael Marquez – Editor

MEXICAN WORD OF THE DAY: METER.
I told her to go to da city so I could METER there.

MEXICAN WORD OF THE DAY: COINCIDE

"I was in di backyard playing and it estarted getting late so my ma'ma told me to COINCIDE"

MEXICAN WORD OF THE DAY: JESTER
I haven't seen my vieja cents JESTER day.

MEXICAN WORD OF THE DAY: CHICKEN WING

If my vieja keeps playing the lottery maybe one day CHICKEN WING

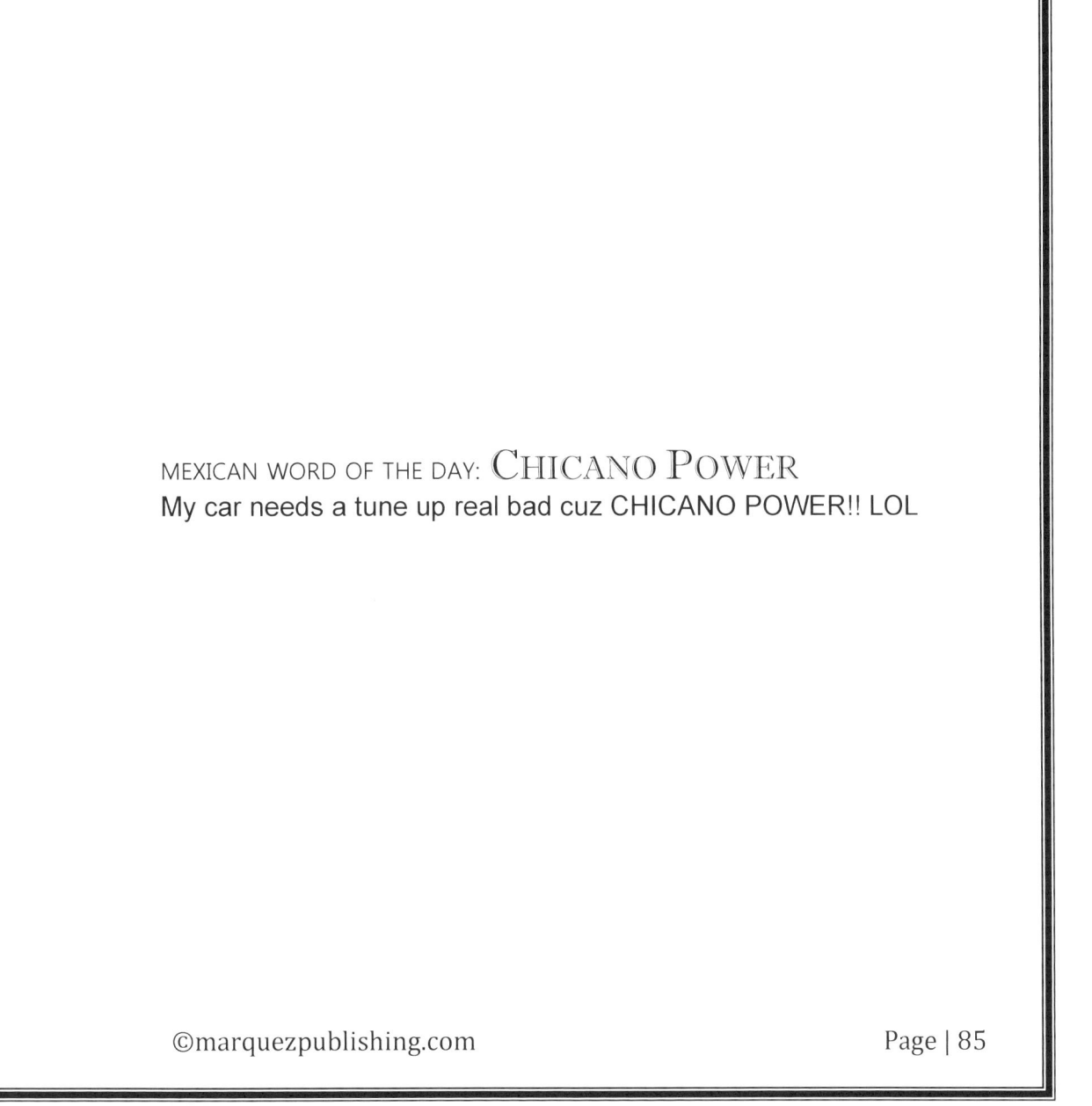

MEXICAN WORD OF THE DAY: CHICANO POWER
My car needs a tune up real bad cuz CHICANO POWER!! LOL

MEXICAN WORD OF THE DAY: CRUTCH

Eee Vato don't get mad but I got a serious CRUTCH on your sister dude!

Rafael Marquez – Editor

MEXICAN WORD OF THE DAY: MOSQUITOES

A lady with 5 kids came into my shop the other day and I had to tell her that YOU MOSQUITOES DAMN KIDS UNDER CONTROL!

MEXICAN WORD OF THE DAY: JUSTICE

My carnal asked me for some money and I said simon but JUSTICE last time puto!

MEXICAN WORD OF THE DAY: CHEST

Oyea Babe, I don't really need it but I'm gonna ask the doctor for some Viagra, CHEST in case

MEXICAN WORD OF THE DAY: SEIZURE

Oyea Vieja Babe… You better hold your skirt down before somebody SEIZURE panties.

Rafael Marquez – Editor

MEXICAN WORD OF THE DAY: CHORES

Eee vato, the economy must really be bad because I have been across the country from CHORE TO CHORE looking for work and I ain't found chit!

MEXICAN WORD OF THE DAY: CHATTER

I locked the keys in my car and had to CHATTER the window so I could get in.

Rafael Marquez – Editor

MEXICAN WORD OF THE DAY: CHIP

We saw this movie last night that had this really cool Pirate CHIP in it.

MEXICAN WORD OF THE DAY: EXPLAIN

Happy Valentine's Day. EXPLAIN to see that you're the only one for me.

Made in the USA
Monee, IL
04 February 2023